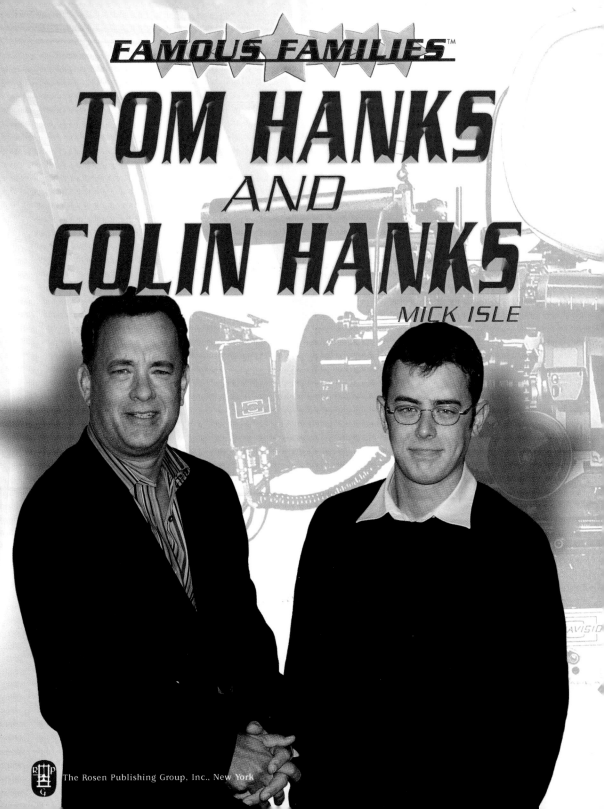

FAMOUS FAMILIES™

TOM HANKS
AND
COLIN HANKS

MICK ISLE

The Rosen Publishing Group, Inc., New York

To Natalie B.

Published in 2005 by The Rosen Publishing Group, Inc.
29 East 21st Street, New York, NY 10010

First Edition

Library of Congress Cataloging-in-Publication Data

Isle, Mick.
Tom Hanks and Colin Hanks / Mick Isle.— 1st ed.
   p. cm. — (Famous families)
Includes bibliographical references and index.
ISBN 1-4042-0266-8 (library binding)
1. Hanks, Tom. 2. Hanks, Colin, 1977– 3. Motion picture actors and actresses—United States—Biography.
I. Title. II. Series.
PN2287.H18I84 2005
791.4302'8'092273—dc22

                                                                2004015542

Manufactured in the United States of America

Contents

OPENING NIGHT

One early evening in January 2002, limousines were pulling up in front of a Hollywood cinema. Flashbulbs popped as a dark-haired, 6-foot, 1-inch-tall (1.85-meter) young man with a boyish face emerged from a car and made his way toward the theater. Those in attendance were taken by how much the young man bore an uncanny resemblance to Tom Hanks. This was hardly a coincidence. The young man was Colin Hanks. Many people were shocked to discover that at this Hollywood premiere of *Orange County*, the film in which actor Colin Hanks had his first starring role, his father, Tom Hanks, was nowhere to be seen. How could Colin's famous dad, one of the world's most popular film actors, snub his own son by being absent on such an important night?

Though it may not seem like it, Tom's no-show is an example of the support and sensitivity he has shown his son ever since Colin first decided to start an acting career. More than twenty-five years in the film industry has made Tom very savvy about the way the business works. He knew, for example, that

Colin Hanks played a young surfer in the 2002 film *Orange County*. Named after the conservative California enclave that also houses Disneyland, Colin's first feature film is set in the same location as the 1982 teenage cult film *Fast Times at Ridgemont High*.

his presence at the opening night of *Orange County* would attract a lot of media attention. Reporters would be bound to focus on the fact that Colin was Tom's son instead of focusing on Colin as an actor in his own right. In order to avoid taking attention away from this important moment in his son's life, Tom stayed away. It is a telling example of how this famous father and his son—renowned for their nice-guy personalities as well as their acting talents—juggle life on and off camera.

Tom Hanks won the 1994 Academy Award for Best Actor for his role as a gay lawyer with AIDS in the blockbuster film *Philadelphia*. The golden Oscar statuette that Tom is proudly holding has been given to each Academy Award winner since 1928—one year after the Academy Awards was established.

CHAPTER 1

MAKING IT "BIG"

Thomas J. Hanks was born on July 9, 1956, in Concord, California. When he was five, his parents separated. Along with his older siblings, Sandra and Larry, Tom went to live with his father, while his younger brother, Jim, stayed with his mother. Tom's father, Amos, was a chef who frequently moved around the country changing jobs. He also often changed wives. Looking back, Tom jokes (in a quote from www.tomhanksweb.com) that by the age of ten, he'd had "three mothers, five grammar schools, and ten houses." Having been constantly uprooted made young Tom very shy. In order to overcome his timidity and make friends at new schools, Tom became the class clown.

Early Breaks

In high school, this love of performance led Tom to begin auditioning for roles in school plays. As he stated in a 1998 interview in *Time* magazine, "I was attracted to acting because it was fun. I'd rather laugh all day long than anything." In fact, he remained so

This is an early photo of Tom Hanks, as he appeared in the 1982 film *Mazes and Monsters*. This movie did not receive good reviews from critics, but audiences had a positive reaction to young Tom.

hooked on acting that when he began college in 1974, he pursued roles in school and in local theater productions. At California State University in Sacramento (where he transferred after two years at Chabot College in Hayward, California), he met and fell in love with an aspiring young actress named Susan Dillingham. It wasn't long before the couple moved in together. Shortly thereafter, Susan—who had changed her name to Samantha Lewes—became pregnant. In November 1977, she gave birth to their first child, Colin. Two months later, the couple got married.

Taking a Chance

Having received good reviews for his work in plays, in 1977, Tom decided to drop out of college and try to make it as a full-time actor. In 1978, Tom and Susan took a chance and moved to New York City. Although both hoped to make it big in the Big Apple, work was hard to come by and money was tight. As Tom told *Time* magazine, "It was a year and a half of horrible scary days." Luckily, after a while, Tom was able to get a manager, who helped him win his first movie role—a part he'd probably rather forget. In fact, today it's hard to imagine Tom Hanks appearing in something as bad as *He Knows You're Alone*—a horror film about a psycho killer on the loose at a bridal party. On the positive side, it did earn him a weekly salary of $785 as well as his Screen Actors Guild card.

Money was still tight until early in 1980, when Tom got his first big break. After many auditions, he landed one of the two lead roles in a new television show called *Bosom Buddies*. This ABC sitcom focused on two friends who work for an advertising agency in New York City. Unable to find an apartment, they dress up as women so they can live in a residence for females. The show was filmed in Hollywood, so the Hanks family moved to California, where Colin's younger sister, Elizabeth, was born in 1982.

Since there were only so many jokes that could be made about men dressing up in women's clothes, *Bosom Buddies* was canceled after two seasons. For a while, Tom did guest roles on popular TV shows such as *Family Ties*, *The Love Boat*, and *Happy Days*. This last opportunity proved to be another big break for Tom since it put him in touch with Ron Howard (who

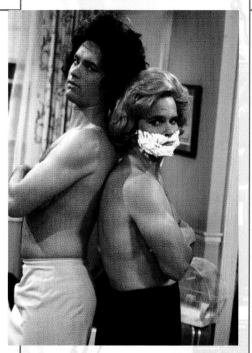

Tom Hanks *(left)* landed a role in the early 1980s TV sitcom *Bosom Buddies*. For the two seasons that the show ran, Tom starred opposite Peter Scolari *(right)*. Tom was widely praised for his hilarious performance on the show.

played the lead role of freckled nice guy Richie Cunningham on *Happy Days*). An actor since childhood, Howard wanted to focus on becoming a director. When he began casting for his next film, he thought of Tom for a supporting role. However, Tom's reading was so good that he got the lead role of a young man who falls in love with a mermaid, played by towering blond actress Daryl Hannah. This original comedy, entitled *Splash*, made big waves at the box office and turned Tom Hanks into a minor star.

A still of Tom Hanks in the 1984 film *Splash*. Tom stars opposite Darryl Hannah in this offbeat romantic comedy. Hannah plays a mermaid who finds herself stuck on land near the Statue of Liberty in New York City. Tom plays her earth-dwelling love interest.

Ups and Downs

Throughout the rest of the 1980s, Tom had constant work in films. He made a series of comedies, most of which were silly, and some of which were quite bad. Even in the worst films, however, critics always singled out Tom for his comedic talents. Though many of the characters he played were jerky or goofy, Tom had originality, humanity, and a sweetness that shone through even the worst material and kept him popular with audiences.

Meanwhile, his determination to succeed and create financial stability for his family meant he was rarely home. Ultimately, his absence led to problems in his marriage to Susan. In 1985, Tom took a break from films so he could be with his wife and children more often. However, despite the increased time spent together, the couple couldn't make things work. Tom and Susan separated in 1985 and their divorce was finalized in 1987. Shortly after, Tom married Rita Wilson, an actress he had worked with in the film *Volunteers* (1985). Tom and Rita had two sons: Chester, who was born in 1990, and Truman, who was born in 1995.

Although many of Tom's early films were financially successful, critics didn't begin taking him seriously as an actor until he won the lead role (after it was turned down by Harrison Ford and Robert De Niro) in a film called *Big* (1998). In this movie, directed by Penny Marshall (another former sitcom star from the popular 1970s show *Laverne and Shirley*), Hanks played the role of John Baskin, a boy trapped in a man's body. *Big* was a major success. It was the first film Tom was in that made more than $100 million. His subtle and complex performance won him his first Oscar nomination.

Saying Sorry

Penny Marshall agreed to give Tom Hanks the role of the grouchy baseball coach in *A League of Their Own* on one condition: in front of costars Madonna, Geena Davis, and Rosie O'Donnell, he had to apologize for the fact that his five previous films had been so terrible.

Unfortunately, the film roles that followed were far from *Big*. For a while, it seemed as if Tom's star was crashing down as quickly as it had risen. His lowest point was the role he played as a spoiled and superficial stock trader in *Bonfire of the Vanities*, a movie that was considered to be one of the biggest bombs in Hollywood history. Luckily, once again Penny Marshall came to the rescue. She cast him in the role of a drunken former baseball star (Jimmy Dugan) who coaches a women's baseball team. For his gruff, tough, and humorous (as well as thirty pounds [fourteen kilograms] overweight, courtesy of his neighborhood Dairy Queen) role, Tom won rave reviews for *A League of Their Own* (1992). The film became the first in a string of hits that has continued to this day. In fact, since *A League of Their Own*, every film Hanks has been in has not only made millions of dollars, but has also received great critical and popular

This still from director Jonathan Demme's 1993 film *Philadelphia* shows Tom Hanks playing the role of a lawyer who sues his firm after he is wrongfully fired because he has AIDS.

acclaim in North America and throughout the entire world.

One of the Greatest Actors of All Times

Tom followed up *A League of Their Own* with a comedy called *Sleepless in Seattle* playing Sam Baldwin, a young widower with a son looking for romance, which he finds with spunky blond actress Meg Ryan. The role allowed Tom to show that he was much more than just a funny guy— he could also be extremely touching and sensitive. Although the film was a great hit, Tom decided to risk his career by taking on an extremely controversial role instead of playing it safe and continuing to do comedies.

In *Philadelphia*, Tom plays a gay lawyer (Andrew Beckett) who is diagnosed with AIDS. When he is fired after his condition becomes known, he hires a lawyer (played by Denzel Washington) to sue his law firm for discrimination.

As it turns out, his lawyer is homophobic. The film was the first Hollywood movie to deal openly with AIDS, homosexuality, and prejudice against gays. The dramatic story was gripping, and Tom's performance was so brilliant that he won the Oscar for Best Actor of 1993. Tom followed up *Philadelphia* with *Forrest Gump* (1994). Once again, he showed his diverse range as an actor by playing a mentally challenged person with a heart of gold named Forrest Gump. Aided by some brilliant special effects, Gump becomes involved in some of the major events of recent American history. Both smart and entertaining, the film won multiple awards, including yet another Best Actor Oscar for Tom. Only once before had an actor won back-to-back Oscars: Spencer Tracy in 1937 and 1938.

After experiencing great success, many actors often hit a slow period in their careers. This wasn't the case for Tom. He continued to take chances by tackling a wide range of original characters. In 1995, he lent his voice to Sheriff Woody, a lively character in the incredibly popular animated feature *Toy Story*. He also teamed up again with Ron Howard to play the part of real-life astronaut Jim Lovell in *Apollo 13*, a suspenseful film about a 1970 space mission that went wrong. Fascinated with space exploration since he was a boy, Tom was thrilled to speak Lovell's famous line "Houston, we have a problem."

In 1996, Tom decided to challenge himself in a new way: by writing and directing his first film. The opposite of a Hollywood blockbuster, *That Thing You Do!* is a lighthearted look back at a young group of musicians trying to make it in the 1960s. Satisfied with this modest success, Tom then returned to mainstream cinema. Teaming up once again with Meg Ryan, the two acted in *You've Got Mail*, a snappy romantic comedy in which a man and a woman fall in love over the Internet.

Then in 1998, along came top director Steven Spielberg with a dramatic role Tom couldn't refuse. *Saving Private Ryan* tells the story of a World War II army captain named John Miller (Hanks) who leads a small group of officers through Nazi-occupied France in search of a missing soldier named Private Ryan (played by Matt Damon). The film, which featured brutally realistic opening scenes of the D-day landings on the French beaches coupled with the terror, suspense, and close camaraderie experienced by America's soldiers left a deep impact on audiences and critics alike. Tom himself was so moved by the story that he broke down and sobbed for more than twenty minutes upon his first viewing of the completed film. *Saving Private Ryan* won five Academy Awards, with Tom receiving a Best Actor nomination as well as a Distinguished Public Service Award from the U.S. Navy. This is the highest honor given to civilians (people not in the military). Both Hanks and Spielberg were fascinated by the research for the film and the true life stories of the World War II soldiers with whom they talked. In fact, in 2001, they teamed up to make the award-winning TV miniseries *Band of Brothers*.

Meanwhile, Tom continued to challenge himself—and his fans and critics—by taking on complex, difficult, and even unsympathetic roles. In *The Green Mile* (1999), based on the book by best-selling author Stephen King, Tom played a prison guard responsible for leading condemned criminals to their deaths. In *Cast Away* (2000), he reunited with director Robert Zemeckis (*Forrest Gump*) to play a workaholic FedEx executive who finds himself stranded on a tropical island after his plane crashes. For the role, Tom lost 55 pounds (25 kg) and grew a long, scraggly beard and hair. Throughout most of the movie, Tom's character, Chuck Noland, battles intense solitude while he tries to stay alive. The only time he speaks is when he pours his heart out to an inflated volleyball that washed ashore with him in a Fed-Ex box. He christens the volleyball, which becomes his cherished companion, Wilson (coincidentally, the name of his wife, Rita Wilson).

Going Nuts

In an interview published on www.tiscali.com.co.uk Tom joked that in real life, he would make a rotten castaway. After a few hours of total solitude, he said, "I'd probably go stark, raving nuts and probably start to do shadow puppets on the wall."

These efforts at taking chances as an actor paid off: Tom received critical acclaim for both movies, including an Oscar nomination for his performance in *Cast Away*. In his next movie, *Road to Perdition* (2002), Tom teamed up with Paul Newman and Jude Law. Tom took on the role of a bad guy for the first time. He played Michael Sullivan, a cold-blooded professional killer who must escape the mafia family he works for when his young son witnesses one of his killings. This role proved to be one of the darkest and most sinister of Tom's career. For Tom, the film was less about violence and more about the complicated relationships between fathers and sons. In composing the character, he drew heavily on his relationship with his own three sons, in particular Colin, with whom he had struggled to maintain close ties after his divorce from Colin's mother.

CHAPTER 2

A LEAGUE OF HIS OWN

When Colin Hanks was born in Sacramento, California, on November 24, 1977, his father, Tom, had just turned twenty-one. Although Tom was still enrolled at California State University, Sacramento, he had just experienced his first professional job as an actor. He was earning $210 a week in a production of Shakespeare's play *The Taming of the Shrew*. He had also just moved in with his college girlfriend (Colin's mother), Susan Dillingham. Shortly after Colin was born, Tom dropped out of college and decided to devote himself to a career in acting.

Dad in a Dress

Colin wasn't even a year old when Tom and Susan (using the stage name Samantha Lewes) moved to New York City. By the time Colin celebrated his first birthday, the Hanks family was living in a small apartment in a run-down Manhattan neighborhood known as Hell's Kitchen. During this time,

Graced with the classic good looks and chiseled features of a matinee idol from Hollywood's heyday, Colin Hanks is sure to achieve showbiz success on his own merits.

the family struggled to make ends meet. Things wouldn't improve until Tom landed his role on *Bosom Buddies*. It was the fall of 1980, and suddenly, Tom was earning $5,000 per episode. Tom, Susan, and Colin moved to California, settling in the San Fernando Valley. Colin's first memories of his father were of a young Tom prancing around on the set of *Bosom Buddies*, wearing ugly dresses and a horrible wig.

Unfortunately, in 1982, ABC canceled the series. Determined to provide for his family and make it as an actor, Tom was afraid to turn down the many early film parts that came his way. Between 1983 and 1987, he worked on seven films. His grueling schedule meant that he was rarely at home, and his marriage suffered as a result. Although he didn't want Colin and his daughter, Elizabeth, to live through the same loss he had experienced when his parents divorced, by the end of 1985, Tom and Susan had separated. In 1987, they were divorced.

Play Time

While Tom stayed in Los Angeles, Colin and his sister, Elizabeth, moved with Susan to Sacramento, where Colin began third grade. In interviews, Colin describes his childhood as normal and happy. In spite of the divorce and Tom's new family with Rita Wilson, Colin saw his father often. He visited him on film sets as well as at Tom's house in Los Angeles, which he came to consider as his second home. Nevertheless, Tom admits in interviews that, at the time, he had no clue how to be a father to Colin and Elizabeth. He has voiced his regret that he was not more active in their lives. Colin confesses that at the

Pictured here, Tom *(center)*, with his wife, Rita, and son, Colin *(right)*, arrive at the 2002 launch party for TriggerStreet.com. Trigger Street is a production company owned by Kevin Spacey, a popular actor who has starred in critically acclaimed films such as *L.A. Confidential* (1997) and *The Shipping News* (2001).

age of thirteen or fourteen, like most teenagers, he went through a phase during which he considered both of his parents to be nerds.

In high school, Colin started performing in school plays. In fact, every year until he graduated, he was involved in a school production. According to Colin (in a January 2002 interview with the *Detroit Free Press*), Tom "always came to my school plays, was always around when I needed him. He had a weird family life as a kid, and both my parents

The television program *Roswell* provided budding actor Colin Hanks with his first dramatic television role.

wanted it to be as normal as it could be." While he was still in high school, Colin performed a series of short one-act plays in a local Sacramento theater. He was thrilled that complete strangers actually paid money to come and see him on stage.

Roswell

After graduating, Colin spent a year at Chapman University in Orange County, California. He then transferred to Loyola Marymount University in Los Angeles, where he studied theater. At this point, Colin didn't really know what he wanted to do with his life. However, he did know that he loved being an actor. When he wasn't study-ing, he was hard at work trying to break into the acting business. Eventually, he succeeded in getting an agent who began sending him to auditions. One of these auditions was for a new television show called *Roswell*. Mixing suspense and science fiction, the show explored the lives of a group of teenagers (some of whom are actually aliens), who share a secret linked to the 1947 crash of a UFO in Roswell, New Mexico.

For two seasons, Colin played the role of Alex Whitman on *Roswell*. During this time, like his father before him, Colin decided to drop out of school. Although sorry that he didn't receive his degree, he figured he was getting an important education by working on the set of a weekly series. Over time, the critically acclaimed show became a cult hit with young fans. Colin's good looks and sweet charm made him a teen heartthrob. Web sites with "cute" photos of Colin began to appear, and he was named one of "America's 25 Hottest Bachelors" by *People* magazine in 2003. In the meantime, he landed some minor movie roles, playing the heroes' best friend in largely forgettable teen films such as *Whatever It Takes* (2000) and *Get Over It* (2001).

Timing is Everything

Because he is always late, Colin Hanks collects watches. Said the young actor (in an interview with *Seventeen*): "I need to know exactly how late I'm going to be—in order to come up with a good excuse."

Orange County

While filming *Roswell*, Colin's agent had given him a script for a movie called *Orange County*. Colin loved it and longed to play the role of the main character. It turned out that the film's director was a friend of his, Jake Kasdan. Though Kasdan had already auditioned hundreds of actors for the lead role, he hadn't found who he was looking for. Then Colin read for the part and proved to be so perfect that he was offered the part that very evening.

The only problem was that Colin couldn't juggle both a starring role in a feature film and the heavy shooting schedule of *Roswell*. At the time, Colin felt he couldn't pass up the opportunity of starring in

In *Orange County*, Colin *(right)* starred opposite Jack Black. Black, a popular comedic actor, is also known as the frontman for Tenacious D, a hard-rock band.

Orange County. Because he felt this way, he had a friendly discussion with the producers of the show, where it was decided that his character, Alex, would be killed off. This occurred when Alex's car collided with an eighteen-wheel truck. His sudden death was such a shock to *Roswell* fans that the producers were bombarded with e-mails begging for Alex's return. Colin himself recalls that it was a very weird experience to "die" and witness his own funeral.

Although he was sad to leave *Roswell*, *Orange County* was an exciting experience for Colin. He played Shaun Brumder, a high school senior and reformed surfer from California's Orange County. Shaun longs to get away from his messed-up family and study creative writing at distinguished Stanford University. Everything goes according to plan until his inept guidance counselor (played by Lily Tomlin) mistakenly sends off another student's high school transcript to the university. Luckily, his slobby, drug-addicted older brother named Lance (the comic Jack Black) decides to step in to help set things right.

Colin was thrilled to be surrounded by a cast that included comedic heavyweights such as Kevin Kline, Ben Stiller, John Lithgow, Chevy Chase, and Catherine O'Hara, as well as Lily Tomlin and Jack Black. In an interview published in the *Detroit Free Press*, Colin said the experience was like "going to comedy school." Even though he was supported by such great talent, Colin felt the weight of being the film's central character. Luckily, however, the movie was a critical success. Reviewers praised Colin for his sensitive performance. They also made a great deal of the fact that he was Tom Hanks's son. The "famous son" phenomenon was highlighted by the fact that both Jake Kasdan and Colin's costar Schuyler Fisk were children of famous Hollywood personalities. Jake's father, Lawrence Kasdan, is the director of acclaimed films such as *The Big Chill* (1983) and *The Accidental Tourist* (1988). Schuyler's mother is Academy Award–winning actress Sissy Spacek.

CHAPTER 3

THAT THING THEY DO!

In interviews, Tom Hanks is always eager to point out how proud he is of Colin. He also admits that he isn't at all surprised that Colin became an actor. Tom recalls seeing his son perform onstage in countless high school theater productions (according to Colin he never missed a single one). As Tom told a *Calgary Sun* journalist in 1999, early on "I knew where he was headed. I saw the talent." Tom is equally proud of his son's determination and drive. "There's a lot of people with talent," he told a reporter for the *Birmingham Evening Mail* in 2002. "But perseverance [determination] is the difference between those who can and those who don't and at twenty-four he's had more jobs than I'd had at twenty-eight."

Fatherly Advice

Tom never tried to dissuade his son from being an actor, but he did warn him about what a difficult career path he was choosing. As Colin recalled in an interview with the *Sacramento Bee*, his father's advice to him was, "Look, whatever you want to do is fine by me. I just want you to really love what you

In this 1995 photo, Colin *(left)* and Tom *(right)* share a private joke at a luncheon honoring astronaut Jim Lovell. Tom played the role of Lovell in the popular 1995 film *Apollo 13*.

Proud Papa

In a 2002 interview with the *Toronto Star*, Tom Hanks described the sensation of seeing his son's performance in *Orange County*. "I was laughing and crying through the entire thing. Understand, when he was five or six years old I was doing *Bosom Buddies*, and he'd come down to Paramount studios, and we'd have lunch and we'd hang out. Now I'm driving back to Paramount and my son's picture is on the side of the soundstage bigger than life, and I'm watching him come down the press line . . . I was both giddy and sobbing with emotion at the same time."

want to do for a living, because there are going to be highs and lows, and if you don't love what you do, those lows are going to be the most excruciating lows you can ever imagine. But if you love what you do for a living, you'll be able to get through those lows and really be able to enjoy the high points." For Colin, it was the best advice he could have received.

Even once Colin began achieving success as an actor, Tom never got involved in his son's career. Tom, Rita, and their two sons live close to Colin, and Colin continues to have his own room at Tom's. However, when they get together, they talk about everything except the projects they are working on. The only aspect of filmmaking Tom does discuss with his son is how to handle the press. As Tom stated in the *Calgary Sun*, "I told him he didn't have to do interviews if he didn't want to. No one ever told me that." Added Colin (in a 2002 interview published in the *Saint Paul Pioneer Press*), "But he also always says that publicity is just as important as making the movie. It feels weird, it's not natural, but you need to do it."

However, when *Roswell*'s teen stars were first introduced to the press, it was precisely because of his famous father that Colin decided not to give any publicity at all. When the show was first launched in 1999, Colin skipped the group interview with the press, fearing that too many questions about his Oscar-winning dad would take attention away from the other unknown actors in the series.

Odd Jobs

Before landing a part on *Roswell*, Colin Hanks got his first taste of professional acting by doing some odd jobs for his father. In 1995, he worked as a set production assistant on *Apollo 13*, in which Tom starred as astronaut Jim Lovell. The following year, Colin had a walk-on (uncredited) role in *That Thing You Do!*, the first (and, to date, only) film written and directed by Tom Hanks. In 2001, he hooked up once again with his dad when he participated in an episode of the HBO miniseries *Band of Brothers*, produced by Tom and family friend Steven Spielberg. Colin played the part of a young American soldier fighting in World War II.

In 2001, Tom signed on as executive producer of *Band of Brothers*, a TV series on HBO about a group of World War II soldiers. *Band of Brothers* got its title from a line in Shakespeare's play *Henry V*: "We few, we happy few, we band of brothers."

First Times

The first film that Tom directed, *That Thing You Do!*, was filmed at Chapman University in Orange County, California. This was where Colin was going to school at the time. Not only did Colin have his first (tiny) acting role, but his college buddies were also hired as extras.

Tom himself directed the episode (for which he won his first Emmy Award for directing).

However, in spite of these early collaborations, Colin claims that the fact that he is Tom Hanks's son has had little to do with his career. As Colin confessed to the *Sacramento Bee* in 2002: "It sounds bad, but my dad wouldn't lift a finger for me." Although Tom was always there to lend his son moral support, he has never become involved in Colin's career or tried to help him. Colin claims to be grateful for his dad's hands-off approach. He confesses that it helped him become a grounded person. He also points out that despite his dad's millions, he has paid his own way since college. "My dad doesn't give me anything," he stated in an interview with London's *Sunday Mirror*. "I buy my own car, and the house I live in is mine . . . [although] he did give me his old mini-van when I was sixteen."

However, Colin is also quick to acknowledge that the famous Hanks name and his strong physical resemblance to his father do carry some weight. Although they don't help him get jobs, they do help him get auditions. Because of the way the entertainment business works, casting agents and producers are especially interested in the children of stars. Colin admits that this curiosity and name recognition has opened many doors. "But," he countered (in an interview with the *Toronto Sun*), "if you can't do anything they're not going to cast you. So I've always felt comfortable with everything I've done knowing that they cast me because they like what I do in the auditions and they think I'm right for the character." He also pointed out that in spite of both his name and his talent, he gets rejected for acting jobs all the time.

"Not a Burden by Any Means"

From the time Tom's children were young, Tom was conscious that although he had chosen a life of celebrity, they hadn't. This meant that Tom was always extremely care- ful to keep his kids out of the

A photo of Colin Hanks at the 2004 Rock the Vote Awards, which was held in Hollywood. Colin was honored for his efforts in increasing voter awareness.

limelight. Nevertheless, Colin learned at an early age to be aware of people who wanted to be his friend only because of his famous father. "I'm a pretty good judge of character and can see through the phoneys," he confessed in a 2002 interview published in London's the *Mirror*.

Meanwhile, during auditions and on the set of a film, Colin admits that he rarely gets flak for being the son of Tom Hanks.

Because Tom has been such an important figure in Hollywood for such a long time, it is logical that many people have worked with him, met him, or heard stories about him. Nonetheless, Colin has found that people respect both his father and the fact that he is trying to make his own way. "They all get it," said Colin in an interview with the *Toronto Sun*. "Yeah, he's my dad and they probably have some stories and some anecdotes that they would love to tell—and they do and that's cool. But they know that I'm my own person and that I've got my own thing going."

More complicated than the attitudes of his colleagues are those of critics and audiences who are quick to look for comparisons between father and son. Having dealt with such reactions for a long time, Colin understands and accepts them, even if at times he gets tired of being compared to his dad. He can also get frustrated that some journalists only want to talk with him about his famous father. "[These comparisons] will die down eventually," he admitted in an article published in January 11, 2002 in the *Toronto Star*. "Really, I've been dealing with this for years, and I got over it a long time ago. I say 'dealing with it,' but believe me, this is not a burden by any means."

In truth, Colin is as fiercely proud of his father as Tom is of his son. This is why Colin stood by his dad at the White House in the summer of 1995 when president Bill Clinton awarded astronaut Jim Lovell (whom Tom had played in *Apollo 13*) with the Congressional Space Medal of Honor for his courage during the failed *Apollo 13* mission in 1970. "America's favorite son" (as Colin was introduced by Tom's friend Steven Spielberg) was also there to applaud his father in June 2002, when Tom won the American Film Institute's prestigious

Jim Lovell *(right)*, the astronaut whom Tom portrayed so well in *Apollo 13*, is shown here receiving the Congressional Space Medal of Honor from former U.S. president Bill Clinton *(center)* in 1995. Tom *(left)* and Colin look on from the back of the room.

Lifetime Achievement Award. Forty-six-year-old Tom, the youngest person ever to have received the award, joked, "If I'm ninety, and I haven't scored another one of these AFI [American Film Institute] things, then I will truly view the latter part of my career as some kind of failure."

Tom
Hanks is
Forrest
Gump

CHAPTER 4

CATCH THEM IF YOU CAN

The year 2002 was a big year for both Tom and Colin Hanks. In two of the year's most popular and critically praised films, Tom displayed the full range of his talents, playing complex characters on both sides of the law. In *Road to Perdition* (for which he was paid a whopping $20 million) he was a mafia hit man. He followed this up with a lighter turn as an FBI agent on the tail of a charming con man played by Leonardo DiCaprio in Steven Spielberg's *Catch Me If You Can*. Teaming up with his wife, Rita Wilson, he then co-produced a romantic comedy that had been rejected by other major Hollywood studios. The modest film, *My Big Fat Greek Wedding*, went on to become the highest-earning independent movie of all time (until it was surpassed by Mel Gibson's *The Passion of the Christ* in March 2004).

Meanwhile, 2002 was a breakthrough year for Colin. He stepped up to play his first lead role in *Orange County*, a film many hailed as the most

In this 2002 photo, director Steven Spielberg *(center)* stands with Tom Hanks and Leonardo DiCaprio on the set of *Catch Me if You Can*. Below is an image from the poster for Tom's 1994 film, *Forrest Gump* (1994).

Family Fun

Tom Hanks recalled that one day in 2002, he and his wife, Rita, were looking for a movie their whole family could see together. The only thing they could find was *My Big Fat Greek Wedding*. Tom joked in an interview published by Knight Ridder, a wire service news agency, "I said, 'Oh, God; we've not only seen it already—we made it.'"

intelligent teenage comedy to have come along in the past few years. Colin said in an interview with the *Detroit Free Press*: "*Orange County* was my first chance to show people that I had some range, that I could be comic and serious, that I could hold the center."

Promising Futures

Since then, both Tom and Colin Hanks have been keeping lower profiles. The year 2003 was the first in a long time in which Tom Hanks was absent from movie screens. Instead, he spent that year and early 2004 working on a variety of film projects that were released in 2004. As an actor, he completed *The Ladykillers*, a remake of a 1950s British comedy about a mismatched group of thieves involved in a big robbery (Tom takes on the role originally played by the great English actor Sir Alec Guinness). In a completely different vein, he then teamed up with Steven Spielberg to play the lead role in *The Terminal*. Based on a true story, this dark comedy is about an immigrant without documents who ends up living in a New York City airport (and falls in love with a flight attendant played by Catherine Zeta-Jones).

Meanwhile, Tom refuses to slow down. In 2004, he began work on *A Cold Case*, a police drama scheduled to be released in 2005. He is also teaming up with Lawrence Kasdan, *Orange County* director, in *The Risk Pool*. In this drama, Tom will play a gambling thief forced to care for his son after his wife has a nervous breakdown. *The Risk Pool* is scheduled to be released in 2006.

As if this wasn't enough, Tom lent his voice to *The Polar Express*, an animated feature released in late 2004. With his production company, Playtone, he has also continued to develop and produce films. His absence from the screen has not resulted in his diminished popularity. On the contrary, in early 2004, Tom was the first-ever recipient of the People's Choice Award for Favorite All-Time Entertainer.

In *The Terminal* (2004), Tom once again pairs up with director Steven Spielberg. This film is based on the real-life story of an Iranian refugee named Merhan Nasseri.

In recent times, Colin, too, has been incredibly busy. In 2003, he played a main role in *11:14*, a suspenseful murder drama costarring Oscar-winning actress Hillary Swank. He also returned to the stage. Alongside other rising young stars, Kieran Culkin and Alison Lohman, he played the role of a spoiled, rich New Yorker in the play *This Is Our Youth*. A thrilled Tom—who has never acted on a British stage—flew to London to see his son perform. Colin said that while his father is proud of him, he's also kind of a bit

Big Bucks

To date, eleven of Tom's movies have made more than $100 million at the U.S. box office. And in the last ten years (1994–2004), his films have grossed more than $1 billion in the United States alone.

jealous—only in the sense that he's so excited that Colin has this opportunity.

Meanwhile, Colin has various projects for the future. He recently completed two very different films that do not yet have release dates. *Standing Still* is an indie comedy about a popular alcoholic actor who reconnects with a group of his college friends years after graduation. *Closing the Ring* is a romantic drama in which the plot moves between Northern Ireland during World War II and North Carolina in the 1990s. In this film, Colin plays alongside famous veteran actors including Shirley MacLaine, Peter O'Toole, and Dennis Hopper. Colin also began work on director Peter Jackson's [*Lord of the Rings* trilogy] upcoming version of the classic *King Kong*. Set to be released in 2005, the film about a giant gorilla on the loose in New York also stars Naomi Watts, Adrien Brody, and Colin's *Orange County* costar Jack Black.

With both father and son branching out in new directions and challenging themselves and their audiences, the only downside in sight seems to be lack of time for certain leisure activities—such as cooking, for example. For Colin, who was hoping to become a "cook type of guy" instead of a "take-out guy," this means that his fridge will continue to be filled with restaurant doggie bags for some time to come.

TIMELINE

1980
- Living in New York, Tom gets an agent. He makes his first film appearance in the trashy thriller *He Knows You're Alone* and earns his Screen Actors Guild card.
- Tom is hired by ABC TV to star in a pilot for a new sitcom, *Bosom Buddies*. He moves to California. The show runs for two years with Tom earning $5,000 per episode.

1983
- Tom is hired by director Ron Howard to star in the romantic comedy *Splash* about a man who falls in love with a mermaid. The film is a great critical and commercial success and makes Tom a minor star.

1984
- Tom makes *Bachelor Party*, a big success at the box office. Over the next four years, he works on six films. Although most earn money, they are not critical successes.

1986
- Tom earns his first $1 million paycheck when he goes to Israel to make the film *Every Time We Say Goodbye*, his first romantic role in a serious drama.

1988
- Tom wins his first Oscar nomination for Best Actor, playing the role of a boy trapped inside a man's body in the film *Big*. A big success with both critics and audiences, it is Tom's first film to make more than $100 million at the U.S. box office.

1989
- After roles in three mediocre comedies, Tom appears as the lead in *Bonfire of the Vanities*, one of the biggest flops in movie history.

1992
- Tom is back on top after he stars in *A League of Their Own*. This film marks the beginning of a string of critical and box-office successes that have yet to let up.

1994
- Tom wins his first Best Actor Oscar for his courageous portrayal of a gay lawyer with AIDS in *Philadelphia*.

1995
- Tom wins his second Best Actor Oscar for his role in *Forrest Gump*. He is the second actor to win back-to-back Oscars ever since Spencer Tracy's wins in the 1930s.
- Tom gets a chance to play the part of his childhood hero, astronaut Jim Lovell, in *Apollo 13*, a film for which Colin works as a production assistant.

1996
- Tom writes and directs his first feature film, *That Thing You Do!*, in which Colin makes his uncredited screen debut as a page.

1998
- Tom wins an Emmy Award for Best Series as the executive producer of *From the Earth to the Moon*, an HBO miniseries he helped produce, direct, and write.

1999
- Tom is nominated for the Best Actor Oscar for his role as Captain Miller in Steven Spielberg's gripping World War II drama, *Saving Private Ryan*. Released in 1998, the film—with shocking footage of the 1944 Normandy invasion—becomes a worldwide phenomenon. Colin begins a two-year stint as Alex, a young outsider surrounded by aliens in the cult TV series *Roswell*.

2000
- Tom loses 55 pounds (25 kg) for his role as a survivor on a desert island in *Cast Away*.

2001
- With his friend Steven Spielberg, Tom produces the HBO miniseries *Band of Brothers*. Aside from an Emmy Award for Best Series, Tom wins a Best Director Emmy for an episode he directed in which Colin played the role of a soldier.

2002
- Tom defies his "nice guy" image by playing a mafia hit man in *Road to Perdition*. In June, he is the youngest person ever to win the American Film Institute's prestigious Lifetime Achievement Award. Tom's production company, Playtone, releases the comedy *My Big Fat Greek Wedding*, which breaks box-office records for an independent film in the United States. Colin makes his debut as a leading man in the comedy *Orange County*.

2004
- Tom is the first recipient of the People's Choice Award for Favorite All-Time Entertainer.

FILMOGRAPHY

Tom Hanks:

1980	• *He Knows You're Alone* and *Bosom Buddie*s (TV series)
1982	• *Mazes and Monsters* (TV)
1984	• *Splash* and *Bachelor Party*
1985	• *The Man with One Red Shoe* and *Volunteers*
1986	• *The Money Pit*, *Nothing in Common*, and *Every Time We Say Goodbye*
1987	• *Dragnet*
1988	• *Big* and *Punchline*
1989	• *The Burbs* and *Turner & Hootch*
1990	• *Joe Versus the Volcano* and *The Bonfire of the Vanities*
1992	• *Radio Flyer* and *A League of Their Own*
1993	• *Sleepless in Seattle* and *Philadelphia*
1994	• *Forrest Gump* and *Vault of Horror I* (TV)
1995	• *Apollo 13* and *Toy Story* (voice)
1996	• *That Thing You Do!*
1998	• *From the Earth to the Moon* (TV miniseries), *Saving Private Ryan*, and *You've Got Mail*
1999	• *Toy Story 2* (voice) and *The Green Mile*
2000	• *Cast Away*
2001	• *Band of Brothers* (TV miniseries)
2002	• *Road to Perdition* and *Catch Me If You Can*
2004	• *The Ladykillers*, *The Terminal*, and *The Polar Express* (voice)

Colin Hanks

1996	• *That Thing You Do!*
1999	• *Roswell* (TV series)
2000	• *Whatever It Takes*
2001	• *Get Over It* and *Band of Brothers*
2002	• *Orange County*
2003	• *11:14*
Yet to be Released	• *Standing Still* and *Closing the Ring*

GLOSSARY

acclaimed Celebrated or renowned.

AIDS (acquired immunodeficiency syndrome) A serious disease caused by HIV (human immunodeficiency virus) that increases an infected person's chance of developing infections and cancers.

camaraderie Companionship or friendship.

controversial An issue or topic that is hotly debated.

cross-dress To dress in clothing of the opposite sex.

D-day June 6, 1944, the day on which Allied forces invaded Nazi-occupied France during World War II.

dissuaded Talked out of, advised against.

excruciating Painful, severe, unbearable.

gross Total profits.

grueling Backbreaking, exhausting.

gruff Rude, fierce, grouchy.

hit man A paid assassin.

homophobic Fear or hatred of gays and/or lesbians.

indie Independent. A word used to describe films, music, or media that is not produced by a mainstream company.

inept Incompetent.

mainstream Standard or everyday.

mediocre Worse than average, inferior.

Oscar An award given annually by the Academy of Motion Picture Arts and Sciences for production and performances in movies.

prestigious Distinguished, important.

Screen Actors Guild A labor union that protects the rights of American actors.

sitcom A funny television program.

snub To treat someone with contempt or purposely ignore him or her.

Spencer Tracy A famous Hollywood actor from the 1930s to the 1960s.

spunky Gutsy, sassy.

subtle Delicate, sophisticated.

sue To take someone to a court of justice to receive compensation for a wrong committed.

uncanny Astonishing, extraordinary.

FOR MORE INFORMATION

Web Sites

Due to the changing nature of Internet links, The Rosen Publishing Group, Inc., has developed an online list of Web sites related to the subject of this book. This site is updated regularly. Please use this link to access the list:

http://www.rosenlinks.com/fafa/thch

FOR FURTHER READING

McAvoy, Jim. *Tom Hanks*. Philadelphia: Chelsea House Publishers, 2000.

Quinlan, David. *Tom Hanks: A Career in Orbit*. London, England: B.T. Batsford, 1988.

BIBLIOGRAPHY

Arnold, Gary. "Film-Star Children." *The Washington Times*, January 11, 2002.

Booth, Cathy. "The Film of the Year. A Perky New Comedy. These Are High Times for Our Most Versatile Actor." *Time*, December 21, 1998.

Cagle, Jess. "Two for the Road." *Time*, July 8, 2002.

"Colin Hanks: 17 Answers." *Seventeen*. February 2002.

Daly, Sean. "Tom Hanks Is the Nicest Hit Man in Hollywood." *Toronto Star*, July 6, 2002.

Day, Anna. "From Under Tom's Thumb; Is Colin Hanks More Than Just Tom's Son?" *The Mirror*, November 8, 2002.

Gardner, David. "Hanks II: My Struggle to Be a Star, by Oscar-legend Tom's Son." *Sunday Mirror*, January 12, 2002.

Gray, Ellen. "Tom Hanks' Son Keeps Low Profile While WB Hypes His New Show." The News Observer on the Web, July 28, 1999. Retrieved April 2004 (http://www.news-observer.com/daily/1999/07/28/day11.html).

Haskell, Molly. "Why We Love Tom Hanks." *Ladies' Home Journal*, April 2001.

Hobson, Louis B. "Like Father . . . " *Calgary Sun*, December 6, 1999.

Jones, Alison. "The Son Also Rises; Colin Hanks Talks Family." *The Birmingham Post*, November 8, 2002.

Kirkland, Bruce. "Happy to Be Hanks." *Toronto Sun*, January 9, 2002.

Kirkland, Bruce. "'Orange County' Has Family Ties," *Toronto Sun*, January 6, 2002.

Lawson, Terry. "Colin Hanks, Son of Tom, Takes the Lead in 'Orange County.'" *Detroit Free Press*, January 7, 2002.

Lawson, Terry. "Hanks examines Family Dynamics as Gangster in 'Road to Perdition.'" Knight Ridder/Tribune News Service, July 9, 2002.

Longino, Bob. "Another Hanks Takes to the Screen." *The Atlanta Journal and Constitution*, January 11, 2002.

McAvoy, Jim. *Tom Hanks*. Philadelphia: Chelsea House Publishers, 2000.

O'Sullivan, Kevin. "I Sat and Sobbed My Eyes Out." *The Mirror*, September 11, 1998.

Parkes, Diane. "You Lucky Guy!: Interview: Tom Hanks." *Birmingham Evening Mail*, January, 20 2001.

Reid, Dixie, "Native Son: Sacramento's Colin Hanks Makes a Name for Himself Apart from His Famous Father." *Sacramento Bee*. January 8, 2002.

"Second-Generation Stars Hanks and Fisk Are Coming Into Their Own." *Saint Paul Pioneer Press*, January 10, 2002.

Soriano, Cesar G. "Colin Hanks Follows His Dad's Lead." *USA Today*, January 10, 2002.

Sullivan, Robert. "It's a Wonderful Life." *Vogue*, December 1998.

Thomson, David. "Profile: Tom Hanks: Adrift on a Tide of Affection." *The Independent*, January 6, 2001.

"Tom Casts His Magic Again." Tiscali.film & TV, Interview with Tom Hanks. Retrieved April 2004 (http://www.tiscali.co.uk/entertainment/film/biographies/tom_hanks_biog/page1).

"Tom on Top." *People Weekly*, August 3, 1998.

Vincent, Mal. "Miracle Mile Oscar Hopes High for Latest Tom Hanks Film." *The Virginian Pilot*, December 10, 1999.

Walker, Robin. "Tom's Son Living on His Own Terms." *Daily Post*, November 8, 2002.

About the Author

Mick Isle is a freelance journalist with a degree in English literature.

Photo Credits

Cover (left) © Steve Finn/Alpha/Globe Photos, Inc.; cover (right) © Globe Photos, Inc.; p. 1 (left) © Karwai Tang/Alpha/Globe Photos Inc.; p. 1 (right) © Nina Prommer/Globe Photos, Inc.; pp. 4, 8, 11, 12, 14, 18, 22, 24, 29, 34 (both images), 37 © Everett Collection, Inc.; p. 6 © Michael Ferguson/Globe Photos Inc.; p. 21 © David Westing/Getty Images; p. 26 © James M. Kelly/Globe Photos Inc.; p. 31 © Clinton H. Wallace/Globe Photos, Inc.; p. 33 © Wally McNamee/Corbis.

Designer: Nelson Sá; **Editor:** Annie Sommers; **Photo Researcher:** Nelson Sá